W9-AXW-926

© Peralt Montagut, 08330 Premiá de Mar (Barcelona) Spain

I.S.B.N. 84-86154-03-1
D.L. B-35077-98
Printed in C.E.E.

The Three

Little Pigs

Illustrated by Graham Percy

There was once an old mother pig who had three little pigs. As she could not afford to keep them all,

she sent them out to seek their fortunes.

The first little pig set off and met a man
with a bundle of straw. He said to the man,
"Please give me that straw so I can
build a house."

So the man gave him the straw and the
little pig built a house with it.

Suddenly, a wolf came along and knocked at the door and said,

"Little pig, little pig, let me come in,"
to which the pig replied, "No, no, not by the
hair on my chinny-chin-chin."
"Then," said the wolf, "I'll huff and I'll puff
and I'll blow your house in."

So he huffed, and he puffed
and he blew the house in
and ate up the little pig.

The second little pig met a man with a bundle
of sticks. He said to the man, "Please
give me those sticks
so I can build a house."

So the man gave him the
sticks and he built a
strong house with them.

Then along came the wolf and said,
"Little pig, little pig, let me come in."
"No, no, not by the hair of my chinny-chin—chin,
I won't let you come in," cried the little pig.

"Then I'll huff and I'll puff and I'll blow
your house in," said the wolf. So he huffed
and he puffed, and he puffed and he huffed
and at last he blew the house in and ate up
the second little pig.

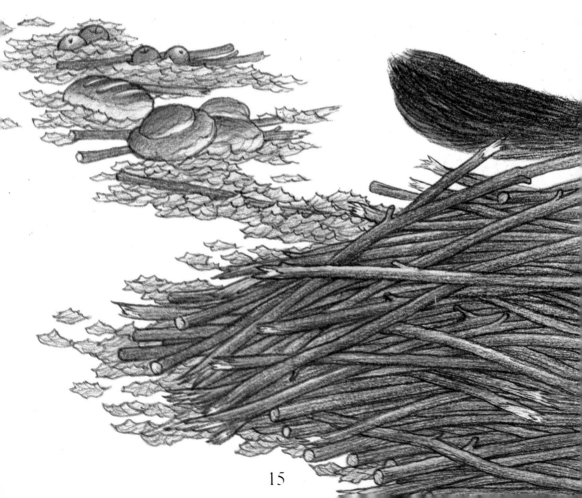

The third little pig met a man with a load of bricks. He said to the man, "Please give me those bricks so I can build a house."

So the man gave him the bricks and the little pig built a very strong house with them.

The wolf could not huff and puff this house down so he said, "Little pig! Let us both go and get some turnips from Mr. Smith's field tomorrow morning at six o'clock."
And the little pig agreed.

But the little pig went to
the turnip field at five o'clock,
so by six o'clock he was back home with
plenty of big turnips. When the
wolf arrived, he was very angry indeed.

Then he thought
of another
plan to trick
the little pig.

"Little pig," said the wolf, "I know where
there is a wonderful apple tree and if you
do not trick me, I will come for you at five
o'clock tomorrow and we'll get some apples."

Well the next morning, the little pig set off
at four o'clock. But this time, because he had
further to go and also had to climb the tree,
he was just climbing down from it when
he saw the wolf coming.

"So you're here before me, little pig? Are
they nice apples?"

"Yes, very nice," said the little pig. "I will throw
one down for you." And he threw it so far that
while the wolf was chasing after it, he jumped
down from the tree and raced home.

The next day, the wolf came again to the little
pig's house.
"Are we going to the fair this afternoon?" he asked.
"Oh yes," said the pig. "What time will you
be ready?"
"At three o'clock," said the wolf.

So the little pig set off early as usual, and
when he arrived at the fair he bought a butter
churn. He was just going home with it when...

he saw the wolf coming.
The little pig jumped into the churn and the churn
rolled down the hill towards the wolf.

The wolf was so frightened that he ran home without going to the fair.

The next day
he went to the
little pig's house
and told him how he
had been frightened
by a great big round
thing that rushed down
the hill at him.
The little pig said,
"That was me
in a butter churn I bought at the fair."

"I got into it when
I saw you and
rolled down the hill."
Then the wolf was very
angry indeed and snarled, "Now I will eat you
up. I'll come down the chimney and get you."
When the little pig saw what the wolf was up to,
he put a big pot to boil on the kitchen fire.

The wolf
came down
the chimney
and... splash
... straight
into the pot.

The pig quickly put the lid on the pot
and that was the end of the wolf.
And the little pig lived happily ever after.